Nonmonogamy and Neurodiversity

MORE THAN TWO ESSENTIALS

Nonmonogamy and
Neurodiversity

Alyssa Gonzalez

THORNAPPLE
PRESS

Nonmonogamy and Neurodiversity

Copyright ©2022 by Alyssa Gonzalez

Thornapple Press
300 – 722 Cormorant Street
Victoria, BC V8W 1P8 Canada
press@thornapplepress.com

Thornapple Press is a brand of Talk Science to Me Communications Inc. and the successor to Thorntree Press. Our business offices are located in the traditional, ancestral and unceded territories of the lək̓ʷəŋən and W̱SÁNEĆ peoples.

Cover and interior design by Jeff Werner
Cover image generated with assistance from WOMBO
Substantive editing by Andrea Zanin
Copy-editing by Heather van der Hoop
Proofreading by Hazel Boydell

Library and Archives Canada Cataloging-In-Publication Data
Title: Nonmonogamy and neurodiversity / Alyssa Gonzalez.
Names: Gonzalez, Alyssa, author.
Description: Series statement: More than two essentials series
Identifiers: Canadiana (print) 20220441979 | Canadiana
    (ebook) 20220442002 | ISBN 9781990869136 (softcover) |
    ISBN 9781990869181 (EPUB)
Subjects: LCSH: Non-monogamous relationships. |
    LCSH: Neurodiversity.
Classification: LCC HQ980 .G66 2023 | DDC 306.84/23—dc23

10 9 8 7 6 5 4 3 2

Printed in the United States of America.

For Tai, who rose to the challenge.
For Rose, who expands my horizons.
For Tsura, who ties my heart.

Contents

Acknowledgments

THIS BOOK WOULD NOT HAVE BEEN possible without the community that defined the words "neurodiversity" and "neurodivergence" and who helped me figure out that I belong among them. It would also have come to nothing without the employers who respected my quirks enough to embrace them, enabling me to build a life that so many of my neurokin never manage. These thoughts are where they are today because of the partners I have loved and who have loved me throughout the years, past, present and future. There is beauty in our strangeness and, thanks to you, I can share it with the world.

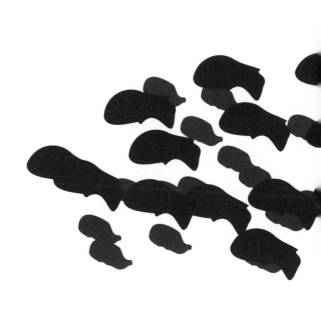

Introduction

Picture it: You've always been weird. Other people's minds are a bit of a mystery to you, or yours is to them, or both.

YOUR ENTHUSIASM IS MORE THAN THEY can handle and it often isn't aimed where other people think it should be. Things that excite them do nothing for you. There are tasks you can do better than they thought was possible. Other activities seem trivial to them but feel impossible for you. Still other things bother you but don't seem to even register for them. Maybe you have trouble noticing when you're hungry or need to use the bathroom. Maybe your sense of taste is so sensitive that you can tell what brand of dried thyme the chef used. Your childhood featured some repetitive comments from teachers and caregivers: "If you would only apply yourself," "is very self-directed and can work independently," "won't sit still," "daydreams too much," "doesn't do homework," "clean your room." You often had stellar grades in some subjects or kinds of work and abysmal grades in others, with teachers scratching their heads at the difference. Maybe loud music has always made you feel alive, or maybe you're so sensitive to sound that you cover your ears when emergency vehicles drive by. Maybe you can't seem to process speech until a few seconds after it's said, leaving friends struggling to understand why you'll ask them to repeat themselves and then, before they're done, respond to the original words. Finding love has probably been a challenge for you, and you may have yet to succeed in a way you find satisfying. You've spent your life feeling like an outsider, existing among the normal folk but never really one of them. You have looked up a variety of terms to try to name the kind of person that you are, perhaps trying on a few ill-defined social ideas like "highly sensitive person" or "empath" or pop-culture concepts like "nerd," or even acquiring a diagnosis of autism, attention deficit hyperactivity disorder (ADHD) or another condition from a professional. In the end, any or all of those terms might feel right, but one name encompasses you and so many more: neurodivergent. This book is for you.

Neurodivergence refers to having a mind that does not work like the minds of other people. The opposite concept is "neurotypicality," and "neurotypical" is a far kinder word than "normal" for such people. People who are neurodivergent experience the world, and themselves, differently than is considered (neuro)typical. Neurodivergence includes differences in social interaction, learning, attention, emotional responses, sensory responses and more. The best-known examples of neurodivergence include autism and ADHD, as well as conditions often associated with them such as dyspraxia (impaired coordination), dyscalculia (difficulty learning math), dyslexia (difficulty with reading)

> The best-known examples of neurodivergence include autism and ADHD

and Tourette's syndrome (sudden, repetitive tics). Other conditions, including borderline personality disorder, post-traumatic stress disorder (PTSD) and dissociative identity disorder, are also sometimes included. The concept of neurodivergence serves to present these situations in a de-pathologized way, as differences that can be understood, managed and accommodated. Our world is one of neurodiversity, in which neurotypical people coexist with people with a variety of neurodivergent minds, forming a beautifully heterogenous medley of humanity. Neurodivergence and neurodiversity do not deny that these conditions can be challenging or even debilitating, or that they sometimes benefit from medical intervention. Rather, these concepts recognize that the conditions are lifelong, often incurable situations that are part of the grand tapestry of human variation and that the people involved deserve recognition, accommodation and support. Neurodivergent people can find value and community in other people with similar mindsets and challenges, and the concept of neurodivergence helps us find each other.

So that's neurodivergence, but what, then, is nonmonogamy? The short version is that nonmonogamy involves pursuing multiple intimate relationships simultaneously with the awareness and consent of everyone involved. Where the normative standard in the English-speaking world usually limits people to a single romantic and sexual relationship, nonmonogamy opens the door to a variety of other models. A nonmonogamous person might have multiple romantic partners at once, considering them all equal claimants on their love and affection. They might live in a shared home with multiple such lovers, practicing "kitchen table polyamory" where the whole group is as intimately close as a couple might be in a monogamous relationship. A pair might be swingers, living as a couple in their day-to-day lives but pursuing extramarital liaisons in a formalized context. A person might live alone but have multiple partners, dating them all separately. A person might have many relationships of different levels of intimacy, or seek out casual connections separate from their romantic relationships, or refuse to assign titles to their relationships and simply let them be whatever they are. Some nonmonogamous relationships include co-parenting children in various combinations or maintaining a household together in various combinations. Some people form groups whose members all love each other in similar ways, while others' partners are not involved with each other. A nonmonogamous person might even fit into several of these categories at once. What unites all of these possibilities is that they refuse the stricture that a person can have only one intimate connection, which must follow a specific "relationship escalator" pattern of ever-increasing enmeshment and union, starting from casual dating and advancing through exclusive dating, marriage, joining of households and finances, co-parenting and so on. Outside the constraints of that model, the possibilities are as boundless as people need them to be, and then some. It is important to note that nonmonogamy is not "cheating" any more than playing rugby is "cheating" at soccer.

Nonmonogamy involves the awareness and consent of everyone involved. This book uses the terms "nonmonogamy" and "polyamory" interchangeably.

Nonmonogamy can feel like a "normal" person's game, not available to neurodivergent people like us. For someone whose mind is not aligned with neurotypical patterns, navigating one intimate relationship can feel like an insurmountable challenge, let alone managing several. To have more than one work at the same time can feel like an impossible dream, or something it does not make sense to even want. The irony, however, is that nonmonogamy is also a minority status, and neurodivergent people often gravitate to the unusual, for reasons as varied as neurodivergent people themselves. We often do not feel the same loyalty to social conventions that neurotypical people do, since those conventions rarely serve us well and often strike us as opaque and confusing. We are often curious about new and exciting ideas. No one quite matches our ability to recognize the parts of mainstream behaviors that don't make much sense and make their less mainstream alternatives appealing. Our priorities often don't match what the mainstream says we should have, which makes alternative lifestyles a natural fit. The sum is simple: polyamory is for neurodivergent people, too.

Why Me?

Nonmonogamy and neurodivergence are personal for me, as a nonmonogamous autistic trans woman who has been active in the neurodivergent community for over a decade. I am published in most installments of the annual autistic-focused fiction and personal essay anthology series *Spoon Knife* by Autonomous Press, and I blog about my experiences as an autistic trans woman, among other topics, at *The Perfumed Void* (the-orbit. net/alyssa). Before a former partner suggested we try nonmonogamy, I had never given the idea much thought. Many of the rules of conventional, monogamous, neurotypical relationships—such as the idea that I should not even *look* at other women once I was in a relationship or that I should feel a need to police my girlfriends' interactions with others to make sure they never crossed into the emotional territory that was "rightfully" mine— never made sense to me. I spent a lot of time confusing partners and would-be partners with this nonchalance, and even more time in frustrated singlehood convinced that I was too weird to love. Growing up in the Cuban-American community in Miami, where loud, bombastic displays of jealousy are seen as a natural, obvious, even necessary part of what it means to love someone romantically, did not make this experience any easier. Once the possibility of another way was in front of me, I took it on eagerly. I found that it fit better with my neurodivergent tendencies than the monogamous, normative template ever could. Recognizing that there were names for who I am and how I operate—"autistic" and "transgender"—was an earth-shaking experience that redefined how I see myself, and it was a similar sort of relief to know that I was not alone in desiring a model of relationships that did not take exclusivity and jealousy as its watchwords. I want to make that possibility more available to others, especially fellow neurodivergent people, and that's why I wrote this book.

How to Use This Book

Too often, the neurodivergent community is marginalized, de-sexualized or patronized. People think of us as vanishingly rare, incomprehensibly weird, tragically childish and fundamentally outside the sexual or romantic spheres of life, or unable to exist as discrete, independent human beings at all. To imagine that we could not only maintain close, intimate relationships with other people, but sustain more than one at a time, strikes many as impossible. Our reality is quite different. The fact that we do not see the world or operate within it as other people do makes nonmonogamy both uniquely challenging and uniquely well-suited to people like us. Many varieties of neurodivergence, if anything, mesh with the requirements of this life more easily than the neurotypical baseline does, and cultivating those traits can make a polyamorous life far easier. However, some situations that come with neurodivergence can make being polyamorous more difficult, and these should not be ignored. This book aims to cover both, providing a primer on the meeting place of nonmonogamy and neurodivergence and how being neuro-divergent can affect how we experience polyamory. Note that I am not a mental health professional and nothing in this book should be construed as a

substitute for the advice of a professional based on your unique situation.

The primary audience for this book
is neurodivergent people considering or
practicing nonmonogamous relationship
patterns. It aims to help neurodivergent
people understand just how well-suited
we are to the polyamorous life and to
help neurodivergent people recognize,
address, manage and overcome the
challenges that being neurodivergent can
bring to nonmonogamy. Secondarily,
this book is also for the partners and
would-be partners of neurodivergent
people, to help them understand the
perspective that their neurodivergent
loves bring to nonmonogamy and to
help them be understanding, accommo-
dating and well-informed partners to
the curious lovelies in their lives. More
than anything, this book aims to make
sure the possibility of nonmonogamous

relationships is as open and available to neurodivergent people as possible, because this gift does not belong to the neurotypicals. It belongs to us all.

Some readers might expect a book like this to be organized by condition, with separate sections for autism, ADHD and so on. This structure would have been counterproductive. Neurodivergence is a concept with fluid, motile edges, and which conditions are included (or not) under its umbrella differs with time and opinion. Similarly, diagnostic criteria, definitions, and even which conditions are considered separate entities from one another often change over time. In 2013, Asperger's syndrome ceased to be recognized as a distinct condition and became part of the autism spectrum, and research is ongoing into the distinction between autism and ADHD, as studies have shown that the original definitions of both were flawed and tangled. Many people bear multiple diagnoses, are unable to access a diagnosis at all but nevertheless feel kinship with neurodivergence, or change diagnoses as they access care. The concept of neurodiversity has room for all of us, regardless of what we are called. Organizing a text like this one by condition would have trapped it in the moment of its writing and rendered it dated as soon as research showed something new.

Instead, this book is organized into two primary sections. One covers various traits and characteristics that neurodivergent people often exhibit and that can make polyamory easier for us, turning nonmonogamy into an opportunity to lead a life better suited to how our minds work. The other covers traits that can make nonmonogamy more difficult for us, with advice on how to manage them. These traits, helpful and challenging alike, appear across a variety of neurotypes (varieties of neurodivergence, such as ADHD or autism) and are equally vexing or vaunted regardless of which neurotype provides them. The diagnostic name of a given person's form of divergence is often less important than the experiences that led them to seek or receive such a name in the first place, and that is given priority here. In this way, readers can seek the advice that benefits their specific situation, unhindered by the clinical winds.

The Opportunities of Nonmonogamy

Nonmonogamy doesn't have a neurotype. Neurotypical and neurodivergent people alike can find that polyamory is the right relationship model for them.

IN SOME WAYS, HOWEVER, MANY neurodivergent people find that polyamory is an ideal fit for how their minds work and how they navigate the world. Polyamory can be a welcome break from the restrictions of the neurotypical world, and with that fact comes opportunity.

You Need Rules to Make Sense

Neurodivergent people often have strong notions of justice, fairness and logic. It is important to many of us that we understand the rules we are expected to obey. That doesn't just mean what behavior is expected or disallowed, but why the rule is in place, what it aims to accomplish and what harms may follow when it is violated. Even if we're inclined to follow rules out of sheer expediency, not knowing the answers to these questions makes it difficult for us to recognize when we've broken them. Neurotypical people are used to these rules and seem to implicitly understand them, picking up on all the unstated premises and assumptions that they struggle to articulate or even recognize when we ask about them. This reality puts neurodivergent people in a difficult position, magnified a thousandfold when the rules in question are about something as intimately emotional as relationships and as difficult to understand a priori as monogamy.

For a lot of us, when we're dealing with unfamiliar rules, the impulse is to beg for detailed clarification, often to the point of becoming annoying or obnoxious. Neurotypical people often think less of us for this habit, imagining it as evidence that we're not as smart as them for not "just knowing" these things. Worse, they also often see this behavior as weaselly and conniving, looking for loopholes and excuses, especially when we start contesting rules that continue to not make sense to us after they're explained or that don't seem to actually address their stated purpose. Monogamous relationships are often premised on drawing lines through classes of behavior, declaring some of it ordinary friendliness and the rest of it as a threatening breach of exclusivity, and the location of those lines can be vague, unclear, fickle and difficult to understand. Is dancing with strangers cheating? How about my close friendship with my ex? My annual camping trip with my childhood friend of a gender I find appealing? Playful banter that some people think is flirtatious? In many monogamous settings, even *asking* about these distinctions is suspicious, as we're expected to either just *know* or to refuse any human interaction we even suspect our partner might dislike. People who need to understand a rule deeply and thoroughly before they can feel confident following it suffer in these situations.

Another common neurodivergent impulse is to flatly ignore rules we don't understand. This provides us a chance to study the situation the rule aims to govern so we can find out how it works, while removing the anxiety of attempting to comply with a rule that doesn't (yet) make sense to us. Some of us might even intentionally undertake actions we think might be "against the rules" to observe the response and confirm that intuition. This is a particularly common pattern when we fear the consequences of asking for clarification, or when asking does not help. To neurotypical people, this often reads as a devious power play, and few things can damage a relationship faster than power plays and the perception thereof.

More anxious neurodivergent people might swear off entire fields of activity if it helps them avoid the terrain governed by rules they don't understand. This tendency can be exploited by abusers to isolate their neurodivergent partners from the outside world, but it can also make non-abusive partners feel like their neurodivergent loves are unduly afraid of how they might react to a perceived rule violation. This strains the relationship with the appearance of mistrust.

In many cases, the part of these rules that feels unjust is not even the behavior they circumscribe, but the very idea that someone could claim to love us while wanting us to change our behavior that much. The notion that someone's desire for us might be premised on changing us to suit their idea of how we should live feels like an insult. When many of us struggle to feel desirable in a world so clearly not made for how our minds work, this perception becomes further evidence that we are far too weird to be loved as we are.

Polyamory provides freedom from these expectations. Almost by definition, nonmonogamy leaves aside common monogamist ideas about relationships, such as norms about not even *looking* at other people of our preferred gender(s), that neurodivergent people often find strange and difficult to accept. Most nonmonogamous relationships accept and even encourage intimacy outside of the couple, rather than being based on a decision that some human interactions are normal and others are threatening. Precisely because it is such a departure from established social norms, polyamory requires people to decide,

together, on the terms of their relationship, and to make those terms make
sense to each other so that everyone
involved knows why they are there and
what they mean. It is not always easy
and it comes with its own challenges,
but for people like us, it can feel natural
in ways that acceding to convention
does not—and that is powerful.

You Don't Flirt Like They Do

It is scientifically established that most
humans are bad at figuring out when
other people are flirting. Even when
dealing with familiar people in familiar
settings, people routinely misread
ordinary friendliness as sexual or
romantic interest and vice
versa. People also have a
bad habit of imagining that

their own interest in someone is mutual as a form of projection. Flirting is a tricky enough topic for monogamous people to navigate when both are neurotypical, often leading to difficult and frustrating conversations about whether various actions "count" and what behaviors they see as a threat to their relationship. But when neurodivergent people are in the mix, navigating all of this gets much, much more challenging.

One of the defining neurodivergent experiences is having our behavior interpreted by neurotypical people in ways that are wildly different from what we intended. Neurotypicals have a habit of reading our wandering eyes as inattention, our practicality as coldness, our shifting moods as dangerous volatility, our need for alone time as hostility, our excitement as sexual interest, and more. Miscommunication is the name of the game in neurodiverse relations, and something most of us must work continuously to navigate. This is perhaps most evident in our flirtation patterns. To put it briefly, neurodivergent people do a lot of things that neurotypical people may read as flirtatious when the intent is anything but. For example, many of us wear our hearts on our sleeves, eagerly sharing the objects of our excitement with anyone who will listen. Some of us get thoroughly and rapidly attached to anyone who seems to share our interest, or who responds by just as eagerly describing their own. We often have different relationships to touch and pressure, feeling grounded when we're under another person's weight because it provides valuable kinesthetic feedback about our own bodies. Many of us avoid eye contact, either in general or with strangers, making our baseline expression seem demure, coy, fearful or simply odd. It is easy for a suspicious neurotypical partner to see any or all of these behaviors as indications of sexual or romantic interest in the other people involved, and in a monogamous relationship, that interpretation can lead to many unwelcome conversations. If the neurotypical partner does not understand or respect that their neuro divergent partner's brain literally works differently than theirs, this miscommunication can end a relationship.

Polyamory sidesteps a great deal of this problem. If you are allowed to flirt outside of your existing relationships, it matters less that neurotypical people will so often misread your behavior as flirtatious. Your friendships can take the form they are naturally inclined to take, all their neurodivergent intimacy intact and not subject to monogamist disapproval. What's more, this choice gives the neurotypicals in your life some non-threatening incentive to figure out what your flirtation pattern actually looks like, so they can cheer you on when you find someone you *do* find that kind of interesting.

You're a Weird Find

Perhaps *the* defining neurodivergent experience is that neurotypical people find neurodivergent people "weird," and they don't tend to hesitate to say so. Many of our childhoods featured ostracism, bullying and clinging tightly to the small number of kind, often also neurodivergent friends we managed to find. Those experiences translate to fraught dating histories as we get older, marked by abundant rejection and steadily eroding self-confidence. It becomes easy to feel unlovable when our neurodivergent quirks, such as flitting attention, verbal tics or difficulty picking up on unstated cues, seem to drive most people away. After a lifetime of this kind of rejection, someone who does decide to stick around feels precious, even if the relationship isn't otherwise a fulfilling match, because *any* relationship provides freedom from that loneliness. Autistic people and people with borderline personality disorder get this treatment most consistently, but it can find any of us, and it is just as unwholesome to anyone.

Neurotypical, monogamist norms tell people like us that once someone decides our weirdness is tolerable, we owe them everything. The alternative is loneliness, after all, and we've already seen how bad that can be. And in monogamous relationships, any need, quirk or pattern that doesn't fit the mold becomes a threat, because if that one partner can't fulfill our needs, they may feel threatened by whoever can. The pressure is on to sever, suppress or deny any personal detail that doesn't fit into that partner's vision. In the monogamous model, a partner is supposed to meet the sum total of our emotional and physical needs, after all, so we are not *allowed* the parts of us that that partner doesn't like. We must shrink, mask, disappear into the role and try to be the neurotypical partner our lover demands, because we are weird finds, right? Expecting any better than that would be foolhardy. In the mainstream, weird people are loved despite, not because of, our weirdness.

But it doesn't have to be like this. Polyamory provides a surprising way out. Maybe a soul mate perfectly matched to every part of us is a vanishingly rare find, but someone who feels good to be around and who enjoys our company in less all-encompassing ways usually isn't. In a polyamorous model, we have the freedom to pursue fulfillment for the various parts of ourselves in *different* relationships, each with their own parameters, each with their own custom levels of attachment. By building a whole support network of love, camaraderie and care, we gain the ability to embody our whole selves *and* experience the intimacy that the monogamist world thinks should cost us far more dearly. The monogamous pressure to find one partner and hold on to them no matter what, on pain of never experiencing that kind of intimacy again, just isn't there. We don't have to be someone else's perfect fit. We can just be, and those who find that properly enchanting can come and go as we and they both please.

You can be as weird as your neurodivergent mind demands, and you will never be too much. That's the beauty of neither expecting nor being expected to be someone's every-thing—or expecting them to be yours.

You Value Your Independence

One of the hallmarks of neurodiver-gence is having ways of living and going about our days that differ from neurotypical expectations. Our traits often include things like sensory sensitivities that make us crave shade and quiet, tight routines that are easy for visitors to disrupt, and difficulty with unexpected changes to our schedules or plans. Some of us maintain our households in ways that can be difficult for others to deal with, whether that means meticulous tidiness or chaotic disorder (or tidiness that only *looks* like disorder). Many of us learn from a young age that depending on other people is a recipe for having our needs dismissed or even ridiculed. Consciously or unconsciously, neurodivergent people often internalize the idea that controlling our life is the only way for it to look the way we want it to look.

In the traditional monogamous "relationship escalator," people increase the level of enmeshment in a relationship over time as a matter of course, moving from dating to combining homes and finances to making binding commitments such as marriage and perhaps having children. This model is not an easy fit for people like us. The expectation that we must cede substantial autonomy to our lover, from joining finances to combining households to even changing our names, can be frightening. After we've claimed what little control over our lives the modern world lets us have, losing any of it, even enough to have someone else's toothbrush in the bathroom, can feel like regression. On top of that, the neurotypical world has a habit of treating any neurodivergent need as silly, frivolous and something to get over or learn to do without. If everything we want or need is an imposition on others, figuring out when a partner is being genuinely unreasonable becomes nigh-impossible.

Polyamorous relationships are particularly amenable to allowing participants to live alone. It is not a rare arrangement for a polyamorous person to maintain their own home and finances and to have multiple partners who also have their own homes and finances. Similarly, in a world where legal regimes place primacy on couples, polyamorous triads and larger groups, especially those sharing a home, have little choice but to negotiate exactly what kind of enmeshment makes sense for them. It can be beneficial to, for example, arrange joint responsibilities for any children in the household but keep finances individualized. Cohabitating nonmonogamous people also have the option to maintain separate personal spaces, such as bedrooms, without the tense conversations that often accompany this desire in monogamous relationships, and this option comes in especially handy if they, say, occasionally bring home non-cohabitating partners. Without the expectation that a relationship must mean the progressive merger of every aspect of their lives, people are free to maintain as much or as little of their autonomy as they wish.

You Thrive on Clear Communication

Something that people in most marginalized groups learn early is that while the mainstream can rely on heuristics and assumptions to guide their actions, we  often cannot. What is intuitive and obvious to them is not so to us, and what is intuitive and obvious to them is unlikely to "just work" for us. People outside the mainstream are forced to construct the ideas that shape our personal realities instead of accepting them from outside, and that goes for neurodivergent and polyamorous people alike.

In practice, this means polyamorous relationships take a special level of communication, above and beyond what it takes to build a relationship that fits within mainstream norms. Without the superstructure of relationship-escalator assumptions, exclusivity by default and preconceived ideas about what it means to be this or that named level of close to someone, the specifics have to be hashed out individually to the satisfaction of everyone involved.

Polyamorous relationships take a special level of communication

For neurodivergent people, this scenario likely sounds familiar. We often have desires and preferences that are unusual enough that the mainstream expects them to be explained. On top of that, many of us take statements literally unless we are primed not to, especially when we are experiencing powerful emotions. The careful, precise communication style that follows is ideal for conversations where common assumptions and heuristics cannot apply and where even seemingly obvious ideas should be laid out in specific language for maximum clarity. For much the same reason that neurodivergent people can excel in technical communication, we can excel at communication about and within polyamory in ways that may surprise neurotypical people.

Precise communication is especially helpful when conversations turn to emotionally difficult topics. It is often important for such conversations to contain clear articulations of emotions unleashed, harms done and responses planned. Conversations about jealousy, in particular, rely on this kind of precision and awareness rather than knee-jerk reactions. Similarly, long-distance relationships, which effectively consist almost entirely of word-based communication in ways that less geographically restricted relationships might not, benefit mightily from not relying on subtext and cultural assumptions. The same skills that get many neurodivergent people branded "cold" and "distant" can become valued assets for fostering closeness and intimacy in a polyamorous setting where they are valued as strengths.

It is worth acknowledging that such communication success is not guaranteed. Even the most logical neurodivergent people still bring their own biases, backgrounds, assumptions and bad habits into their relationships, to say nothing of how many of us turn our heuristics for interacting with the neurotypical mainstream into ingrained patterns we might struggle to set aside even when they're not appropriate. Mismatches between these assumptions can lead to hard conversations about what agreed-upon terms actually mean and what people actually expect from each other. Nonmonogamy creates a space where such clarity is mutually regarded as critically necessary and, therefore, where carefully going over the rules together is likely to be welcome rather than suspicious.

The Challenges of Nonmonogamy

It might seem that nonmonogamy and neurodivergence go
together like peanut butter and
jelly. In many ways, they do.

HOWEVER, BEING NEURODIVERGENT
also presents many challenges for a
polyamorous lifestyle. Getting the most
out of the freedom and possibility of
polyamory requires that neurodivergent
people grapple with these difficulties

and find solutions, mitigation techniques and partners willing to respond helpfully when these scenarios arise.

Rejection-Sensitive Dysphoria

Contrary to the popular perception of many neurodivergent people as cold and unfeeling, many of us have bigger, louder feelings than we often understand or know how to resolve. One of the most difficult emotions for us to grapple with is rejection-sensitive dysphoria. This classically ADHD experience makes ordinary experiences of rejection and disapproval feel like wholesale referenda on our value as people. It is difficult to overstate how intense these feelings can be. In the throes of rejection-sensitive dysphoria, a person can switch instantly from an ordinary mood to deep despair or vocal rage, and this experience can even be physically painful. At their worst, these disproportionate responses can resemble mood disorders, and people with borderline personality disorder can have similar reactions. These intense emotions make it difficult to think or communicate clearly and can spawn unhealthy coping mechanisms, including avoidant attachment, substance abuse and self-harm.

Rejection-sensitive dysphoria is difficult enough to deal with for people on their own or in monogamous relationships, but it presents additional challenges in polyamorous settings. For the time being, polyamory remains outside the norm and monogamous people are rarely inclined to keep their opinions about it, or about people who participate in it, to themselves. People with rejection-sensitive dysphoria often become people-pleasers, invested in others' approval at the expense of their own desires, and moving counter to the mainstream can be difficult for them. Additionally, seeking multiple partners necessarily means we will experience more rejection than someone seeking only one. In addition to having to weed out anyone for whom our polyamorous status is a dealbreaker, we may end up continuing to seek even after finding our first partner, creating additional opportunities to be turned down. Rejection is hard for everyone, but when it feels like a judgment that we are entirely worthless, it becomes a particularly unwelcome experience.

Jealousy is another especially vexing emotion in the context of rejection-sensitive dysphoria. What could be a manageable flash of negative emotion for others becomes an overwhelming tide, convincing the sufferer that their partner has already abandoned them and everything else is a formality. When every momentary displeasure becomes magnified in this way, it is difficult for a relationship to feel stable, safe and healthy, and any experience of approval and respect can become fleeting and hard to retain.

Within relationships, rejection-sensitive dysphoria can make it difficult to have conversations about challenging topics. If one person's behavior is causing the other distress, rejection-sensitive dysphoria can magnify its impact regardless of which person's behavior is at issue. It can lead to people withdrawing from one another, hiding difficulties that would be better addressed and walking on eggshells to try to prevent an episode. Clear, accurate communication is the foundation of any successful relationship, particularly one that defies

It is important for people who deal with rejection-sensitive dysphoria to be aware of their condition and have tools for managing it.

societal norms, so it is important for people who deal with rejection-sensitive dysphoria to be aware of their condition and have tools for managing it. Being able to recognize when our emotions are more intense than a situation warrants and to manage the gap between our interpretation and the reality of the situation can mean the difference between feeling successful in polyamory and feeling like it could never work.

Rejection-sensitive dysphoria is a neurological, genetic condition that is part of ADHD and other forms of neurodivergence. It has no cure, but it can be managed. There are many approaches to managing rejection-sensitive dysphoria, and any or all of the following might be helpful for keeping it in check.

AFFIRM YOUR VALUE

Even when things look unpleasant or grim, you are still the same dynamo of wondrous possibility you were before. You would not have gotten as far as you have if you were truly worth as little as your rejection-sensitive dysphoria says you are. Find some personally resonant statements that you can use to crowd out inaccurate messages your dysphoria is sending you. "I am allowed to make mistakes" and "I am stronger than I think" are good starting points.

EMOTIONS ARE WHAT THEY ARE

Emotions are not good or bad on
their own; they simply are. At their
best, emotions provide information
about how situations are affecting us,
information that can guide our actions.
This is still true when those emotions
seem far more intense than they should
be. Exercise mindfulness so that you
can name them accurately, let yourself
feel them in places of safety, and share
them with people close to you so that
they can help you work through them.

CHOOSE UNDERSTANDING PARTNERS

It is critical that people close to you,
especially your partners, know that you
struggle with rejection-sensitive dysphoria. Your loved ones cannot respond

appropriately to your situation if they do not understand it. People who can respond compassionately to your difficulties are worth their weight in gold.

TAKE TIME TO PROCESS

Rejection-sensitive dysphoria is, effectively, a failure of perspective. Your emotional centers are treating what are likely relatively small trials as huge events. You have the ability to take a deep breath and insist on some time to process things that feel that debilitating. That time can put some distance between you and those large emotions, enabling you to process them more accurately. With enough time to get away from the immediate sting of a rejection, you can effectively wait out some of your dysphoria response. Patience is protective.

FACE YOUR FEARS

One of the counters to the catastrophizing of rejection-sensitive dysphoria is proving to yourself that the situation is not as bad as it looks. Facing fears provides direct, personal evidence that they are not as dreadful as they seemed at first, which you can then use to remind yourself that similar future situations are also not as bad as they look.

SEEK PROFESSIONAL ASSISTANCE

Rejection-sensitive dysphoria responds to some medications and talk-therapy techniques. With the assistance of a

mental health professional trained
in the use of these tools, you can
reduce its impact on your life.

Alexithymia

Many neurodivergent people struggle
with naming their emotions. This
does not mean that we don't *feel* our
emotions, although our experiences
and responses often vary dramatically
from neurotypical expectations. Rather,
connecting events to physiological
responses, and those responses to
specific, named emotions, can be challenging for some neurodivergent people.
This condition is called alexithymia,
from the Greek for not having words
for our emotions, and it poses some
significant challenges in relationships.

All relationships are improved when a person understands their emotions well enough to name them, but this can be especially true for polyamorous relationships. Polyamorous relationships present unusual situations that require careful processing and conversation. It takes a certain understanding of our own patterns and needs to capably navigate the feelings that might come up when our partner's partner is visiting for dinner, or during a conversation about scheduling date nights with multiple people, or when we consider why seeing our partner take their new lover to that restaurant the two of you used to enjoy but haven't been to in a long time might not feel good. Alexithymia can mean that most negative emotions seem to blur together into an anxiety-flavored mélange, or that anger, excitement and anxiety are difficult to distinguish because they all involve an elevated heart rate. Outward signs of emotion, such as facial expressions, can be similarly mixed, limiting others' ability to read our emotions and relay that information.

Alexithymia limits our ability to effectively advocate for our emotional needs. Recognizing the emotions we're experiencing is a key step in knowing what incited them, what is causing them, and how they can be effectively and equitably addressed. Managing alexithymia is a process of building awareness, and several practices can be useful.

- **Read literature.** Narratives such as novels and short stories feature characters experiencing emotions in context, often clearly described. For much the same reason that stories are such a key part of how humans relate to one another, to their world and to their societies, experiencing stories can help you build a more complete awareness of what emotions look like, how they feel and what situations usually incite which emotions, helping fill the gaps in an alexithymic brain.

- **Count your heartbeats.** There is limited clinical evidence that learning how to accurately count your own heartbeats, in both calm and agitated situations, can reduce anxiety and improve awareness of your emotions.

- **Get creative.** Taking up a creative hobby, such as writing, painting or composing music, can help build emotional awareness, since these hobbies often rely on and train that awareness as part of their practice.

- **Start a journal.** Even if you're not interested in becoming a novelist, writing about your daily experiences can help you process emotions that are currently difficult to name, growing your ability to recognize them. It is important that this journal be more than a mere recounting of the day's events; make an effort to also include some rumination about the emotional matters you experienced.

Alexithymia is a genetic, neurological condition that can be part of the neurodivergent package. Addressing the challenges that it brings to your life starts with becoming aware of its impact. Properly managed, it

does not have to be an impediment
to living in polyamorous bliss.

New Rules, New Lines

Many neurodivergent people thrive
on clear lines, obvious rules and hard-
and-fast distinctions between different
ideas. Few things in this world truly
line up with such categories, but the
ones that do become lodestones we can
use to navigate the rest. For this sort of
mindset, the rigid norms of monogamy
can be comforting. Declaring certain
behaviors off-limits outside a single
romantic or sexual connection makes
the distinctions between different kinds
of relationships stark and easily seen,
which makes all those relationships
potentially easier to navigate. In a
terrain as potentially variable and

volatile as human relationships, that kind of stability can mean a lot to us, even if we don't necessarily find all the restrictions sensible on their face.

Polyamory asks people to start breaking down those rigid patterns. What if a connection outside our existing intimate relationship doesn't have to mean that relationship is doomed? What if romantic acts were not restricted to a single pair? What if jealousy does not automatically mean our partner has done something wrong? These questions remove pillar after pillar from the edifice of monogamy, forcing us to interrogate their purpose and value and, usually, find them wanting. The resulting loss of structure can be frightening to those of us who relied on those old, strict definitions to provide stability for our world.

One loss that can be especially tricky to navigate is the shifting distinction between romantic or sexual partners and friends. In a monogamist world, many acts of affection and care between friends are stigmatized or barred as part of the very definition of an exclusive partnership. Absent that sense that engaging in such acts would be a threat to our romantic relationship, what stops us from enjoying the simple comfort of curling up in a friend's arms to watch a movie or telling our friends we love them? If we do partake of such actions, what keeps our romantic relationships distinct from the others?

Similarly, if monogamist hard lines like "cheating" no longer mean the same thing in polyamory, what determines when a relationship should end?

How much fixing should a relationship seem to need before it is better off scrapped? How do we figure out that we might work better as friends, if the activities among friends seem more and more like what used to be just for romantic or sexual connections?

The key lesson here is that reevaluating rules is not *just* a loss—it's also a *gain*. With the shedding of old definitions and ideas comes the installment of new ones in their place. The point of this whole exercise is the freedom to follow our hearts wherever they may lead and to negotiate our realities with openness and honesty. This can mean defining our romantic and sexual connections in new ways, such as:

- My partners are the people for whom I routinely buy holiday gifts.

- My partners are the people whose families it's important for me to know.

- There are certain activities I only share with my partners, or with specific partners, such as my first watch of a specific show or movie they like.

- My partners are the people with whom I use pet names.

- I live with my partner, but we both pursue casual connec-tions with other people.

- My partners are the first people I ask to help me with life challenges, such as moving, job loss or illness recovery, and I'm one of the first people they ask.

- My partners are the people who help me with my deepest emotional difficulties, the ones I might not share even with my close friends.

- My partners are the people whose anniversaries with me I celebrate.

Losing the stability of conventional definitions does not have to be destabilizing. It is an opportunity to make the rules we live by reflect what actually matters to us.

Hell Is Other People

In addition to being one of the more quotable of Jean-Paul Sartre's aphorisms, this line often describes how neurodivergent people feel about mainstream society, or

parties, or dating, or any other time when we are expected to mingle with large numbers of neurotypicals. There are a lot of reasons for this reaction. Mainstream society is often not kind to people it sees as strange or deviant, and neurodivergent behaviors are a perennial butt of jokes in mainstream entertainment. Polyamorous spaces are not immune to this pattern and navigating it is never pleasant. Neurotypical people often slot neurodivergent people into an archetype in the dating sphere, which can be unpleasant for everyone involved.

Mainstream society is often not kind to people it sees as strange or deviant.

The Manic Pixie Dream Girl archetype in film is a young, attractive woman whose unusual mind, free spirit and youthful naïveté combine to make her a foil for a staid, usually neurotypical man. Her role is to drag him out of his boring life and into cute adventures and wild sex, while seemingly expecting nothing from him in return. Some people expect their neurodivergent partners to behave this way in real life, which is not fair to either person. This archetype becomes frustrating because people who expect their partners to be like this tend not to react well when those partners turn out to have ordinary human needs or ambitions or otherwise exist outside of injecting whimsy into someone else's life. Although "manic pixie dream boys" exist as a concept, in practice this archetype is strongly gendered and it is much rarer for neurodivergent men to be perceived this way. Couples "looking for a third" sometimes make a bad habit of prioritizing finding a partner who fits into this archetype, and the resulting drama can be unhealthy for a neurodivergent person to inhabit.

THE ROBOT

Another stereotype applied to neuro-divergent people, most consistently autistic people, is that we are so cold, robotic and obsessed with our specific interests that we cannot provide any human warmth in a relationship. This stereotype is damaging on more levels than can be adequately laid out in a single paragraph. It can lead to people dismissing our logic as alien and not worth considering by anyone else. It can lead to people refusing to recognize our emotional displays until they rise to a neurotypical-approved intensity. It can lead to people dismissing our polyamorous status entirely because "of course someone that reptilian and inhuman would think that's acceptable." We can be perceived as too unfeeling to be anything but a casual hookup, or too passionless for casual hookups, or unsuited to being around other people at all—all on the basis of our neurodivergence. It is one of the more dehumanizing ways that people can treat us.

THE TERROR

Some people are afraid of us. Some people hear the name of our neurodivergence and immediately reach for harrowing accounts of interpersonal abuse. They imagine neurodivergent people in general, or people with specific named conditions, as volatile powder kegs or calculating manipulators, liable to drive their partners mad with contradictory moods or relentless gaslighting. Often, people will picture someone utterly inflexible about anything they decide is important or unwilling to consider anyone's needs but their own. A neurodivergent person could fit any or all of these descriptions and their neurodivergence might contribute to how they exhibit these traits, but being neurodivergent does not *make* a person be or do these things. Abusive, manipulative, volatile, inconsiderate people exist across neurotypes, including among the neurotypical, and the consistency with which the neurotypical mainstream attributes these traits to us amounts to an especially hurtful stereotype.

All varieties of neurodivergence may be characterized in this unfair way, but people with borderline personality disorder are particularly likely to experience this treatment. Borderline personality disorder is characterized by rapid and extreme mood swings, a powerful fear of abandonment, an unstable sense of self and paranoid episodes, all of which are much more dramatic without mental health support or treatment. It is not without reason that a condition with such a pattern could become connected to hurtful or abusive behavior in the popular imagination, but it is also not a given that someone with this condition will be an abusive or otherwise unhealthy partner. Indeed, an astute reading of that list of symptoms will reveal that it also makes someone especially vulnerable to abuse. People with borderline personality disorder, perhaps more than most other kinds of neurodivergent people, are vulnerable to gaslighting, trauma bonding, and a variety of other emotional abuse tactics *because* of the very symptoms that the mainstream assumes makes them natural abusers. Fear of abandonment can make a person cling too tightly to a lover, but it can also make them avoid getting too attached at all or comply with dangerous requests if it means their lover will stay.

Borderline personality disorder might be the most dramatic example, but this general pattern holds across forms of neurodivergence. The neurotypical mainstream fears what it does not understand, which makes it treat us all like terrors instead of recognizing abusive behavior for what it is. The

irony is that most neurodivergent people
are used to bending over backwards
to fulfill others' expectations and
find having to advocate for ourselves
to be exhausting and sometimes
unfamiliar terrain, making us statis-
tically overrepresented among abuse
victims while the mainstream accuse
us of being natural perpetrators.

THE WEIRDO

When all else fails, neurotypical people
have a habit of just thinking we're
weird and escalating that confusion to
discomfort, fear, hostility or disgust.
This reaction often occurs long before
any disclosure of neurodivergence on
our part. For many of us, this is the
background radiation of being alive and
barely registers anymore, and it makes

dating especially frustrating. People who perceive us this way are particularly unlikely to react well to any request for accommodation, such as a call for dimmer lights or clearer language.

The frustration of others' expectations is not easily transcended. People bring what they bring to interpersonal interactions, and sometimes that includes incorrect or bigoted ideas about what it means to be neurodivergent. Most of them can be educated, but it is not up to any one neurodivergent person cornered into an unpleasant interaction to do the educating. This situation does not have an easy solution. In the end, all we can rely on is our capacity to advocate for our needs, recognize unpleasant situations before they become too difficult to escape, and accept that sometimes, other people won't like us.

Conclusion

THE NEUROTYPICAL MAINSTREAM rarely has anything kind to say about us. Too often, they see us as deviations and mistakes in need of correcting, curing and worse. Our strangeness is something they cannot or will not accept, and most of us have memories of childhood bullying or adult bigotry to testify to that reality. As the autistic joke goes, we were "born on the wrong planet," thrust into a world invested in its own notion of "normal" that often seems disinclined to make space for those who don't fit that idea. And space travel is a distant dream.

But what we are is something altogether more beautiful than that hateful assessment would suggest. We hold up a mirror to the neurotypical mainstream and dare it to look at itself. It is a rare moment indeed when the mainstream accepts any insight from us about the strangeness it calls normal, or the normalcy it calls strange. The beauty of our minds is that we get to know this reality even as they refuse it. We are wired differently. Our reactions to various situations are different, our needs are different, our learning is different, and more—and there is beauty in our strangeness. Our very existence (neuro)diversifies our world, adding wonder and excitement to the landscape

Why *wouldn't* people want to date us?

of human minds. Our differences make us who we are, and who we are is amazing. Why *wouldn't* people want to date us? Why wouldn't *lots* of people want to date us?

Too often, that mainstream would have us imagine that there is no place for us in any human endeavor, and nonmonogamy is no exception. Everything that makes us unusual and interesting becomes something that, to them, makes us confusing and unlovable. That's where they're wrong. Not only does polyamory not belong to a specific neurotype, but the very things that make us so distinctive can make a nonmonogamous relationship model a better fit for us than it is for a lot of them. So many of us have traits, from a need for rules to make sense to a deter-mined independent streak to unusual flirtation patterns, that lend themselves to this life, and many of us are far happier being nonmonogamous than we ever were looking for a soul mate to ride the relationship escalator with us.

It is not an easy path, even if it is one we can enjoy far more than the alternative. Our challenges are a package deal with the opportunities, and enjoying the delights that polyamory has to offer means coming to grips with them. Polyamory means deconstructing rules that might have been comfortable demarcations between otherwise fuzzy ideas, confronting more bigotry than you otherwise might have, dealing with new and unfamiliar emotional cocktails, and feeling the intense unpleasantness of rejection-sensitive dysphoria. Living this life to its fullest potential means finding ways to cope with and transcend these challenges, whatever that looks like for you. Most of these tools are helpful even for people content with a single intimate relationship, because they foster what so many lives desperately need: deep inner awareness and intentional life choices.

In a just world, the mirror we present to the mainstream would lead it to reexamine itself with that same intentionality. The destructive power of jealousy would be acknowledged and taken seriously instead of treated as a cute little sideshow or a sign that someone's love is "real." Rules would be explicit and packaged alongside every detail required to understand them. The edges of relationships would require no policing, for they could simply be whatever they are. Hints and whispers would give way to people simply saying what they mean to each other and receiving it in kind. And, to venture outside the relationship sphere, none of us would be put through the peculiar anti-neurodivergent hell that is job interviews. We will never get that world, but we can build a facsimile of it in our relationships, and that might be the most beautiful thing we as neurodivergent people ever do, whether for each other or alongside neurotypical friends, partners and intriguing baristas who flirted back that one time.

Neurodivergence and nonmonogamy go together like autistic people and collecting things, like ADHD people and sleeping in, like borderline people and loving loudly and deeply: better than anyone but us could ever really understand, even if it's not always easy. With awareness of our specific challenges and capabilities, no version of neurodivergence or neurotypicality need be an obstacle to a lively and fulfilling experience of polyamory. Good luck!

Glossary

Monogamist: Of, relating or pertaining to monogamy as a social institution, especially the ideas that underlie and help sustain monogamy as a social institution.

Monogamy: A relationship model with two participants who are limited to that single romantic and/or sexual relationship, and in which the desire for or establishment of an extra-relationship connection is typically seen as breach of the relationship's terms and a reason to call its future into question. As an adjective, **monogamous.**

Neurodivergence: The condition of having a mental or cognitive variation outside the norm, such as autism or dyslexia. As an adjective, **neurodivergent.**

Neurodiverse: A descriptor for a group or setting containing multiple distinct neurotypes. Analogous to "racially diverse."

Neurodiversity: A movement and idea that recognizes that not all brains think or feel the same way and these differences are natural variations in the human condition. Analogous to "racial diversity."

Neurotype: A specific mental variation, such as autism or ADHD, with definable characteristics and patterns.

Neurotypical: Of typical intellectual, mental and cognitive functioning. Often indelicately and imprecisely termed "normal." Opposite of **neurodivergent**. As a noun, **neurotypicality**.

Nonmonogamy: A relationship pattern in which no participants are limited to a single sexual and/or romantic relationship, and everyone involved may pursue more than one such relationship with the awareness and consent of all participants. Here used as a synonym of **polyamory**. Opposite of **monogamy**. As an adjective, **nonmonogamous**.

Relationship Escalator: A relationship pattern common in monogamous relationships in which the participants are expected to steadily merge and intermingle more and more of their lives, often through steps such as cohabitation, establishing joint finances, getting married, and raising children together. Although the order of the steps is often variable, a defining feature of the escalator is the expectation of more steps and viewing resistance to taking them as a sign of immaturity or lack of commitment to the relationship.

ALYSSA GONZALEZ IS A BIOLOGY PH.D., public speaker and writer. She writes extensively about biology, history, sociology and her experiences as an autistic ex-Catholic Hispanic transgender immigrant to Canada at her blog, *The Perfumed Void*. She also writes speculative fiction that explores social isolation, autism, gender, trauma and the relationships among all of these things. She lives in Ottawa, Canada with a menagerie of pets.

About the

MORE THAN TWO ESSENTIALS SERIES

More Than Two Essentials is a series
of books by Canadian authors on
focused topics in nonmonogamy. It is
curated by Eve Rickert, co-author of
*More Than Two: A Practical Guide
to Ethical Polyamory* and *Polyamory
and Jealousy*, the first book in the
More Than Two Essentials series.
Learn more at morethantwo.ca.

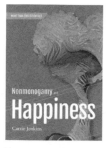

**Nonmonogamy
and Happiness**

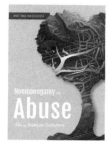

**Nonmonogamy
and Abuse**

**Nonmonogamy
and Teaching**

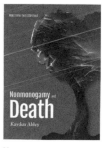

**Nonmonogamy
and Death**